To Susan
— Peace —
Joanna

TO BETHLEHEM

*Christmas
in Poem and Story*

*by
Joanna M. Weston*

this book is for
Robert
with love

© 2015 Joanna M. Weston

All rights reserved. No part of this publication may be reproduced, stored in a retrieval system, or transmitted in any form or by any means, electronic, mechanical, photocopying, recording, or otherwise, without the prior written permission of the author.

Printed by CreateSpace

ISBN 978-0-9938287-3-7

Published by
Clarity House Press
2015

INDEX

Advent 1

Christmas 33

Epiphany 71

Acknowledgements 101

Biography 103

ADVENT

THE MARY WINDOW

she's held
in stained glass

young woman
captivated by
wide-winged angel

head bent
she listens
oblivious to
her background
of desert hills

she   focal point
of angel
king and shepherd
unaware of them all

she steps
from the frame
into our lives

THE ANGEL

light comes winged
dazzling   a shape
that brings words
from God
of a child to come

the mother
trembles
at the vision

who is she
to doubt
to question
when God speaks

THE TIME

when the sun flares
scarlet tongues of fire
then our God
comes

when the moon weeps
blazing yellow sparks
then our God
comes

when the stars write
as white hot embers
then our God
comes

when all creation pulses
with the beat of running flame
then our God
is here

THE MOTHER'S STORY

    Vegetable stew to be made … Mary put the bowl in the wrong place … Should I believe this story she tells? Peel the eggplant … … … my daughter talking of angels and pregnancy – and pregnant she surely is. I wouldn't have believed it of my Mary but she's filling out, her bleeding stopped.
    She's a good girl, I know she is, all set to marry Joseph – a nicer boy you can't imagine, with good living from his carpentry, I couldn't have asked for better for Mary if I'd tried. He says he loves her, but whether he'll marry her now is another question.   >>>

Should I talk to him? What should I do? I don't know which way to turn.

Some of the women think it's funny: they snigger behind their hands when they see me coming. I can imagine the gossip round the well.

Where's the garlic? Did she put it away yesterday? I saw it last night – no she didn't – and there it is!

What am I to do? I can't hold my head up for the shame of it.

It's a good thing my poor husband is dead --- he'll turn in his grave at the disgrace on the family. And disgrace it is.

But Oh – if she should be stoned to death! Dear God in heaven – I daren't think about it. If only Joseph will marry her.

What am I to do? Who will save her? >>>

She came to me yesterday with a tale of an angel and it being a child of God, to be called some fancy name … I hoped and hoped she'd gained weight – and now this story.

I've not put pepper in – there it is.

If only the synagogue doesn't rule against her … if only Joseph will marry her … there's been no other man round her since Joseph came on the scene last year. Oh dear! What am I to do? Or think? Angels! I ask you! There has to be a better story than that.

Olives in the yogourt side dish and it's ready. And yes, I will talk to Joseph; see if he will marry her. Make him marry her. My Mary shan't be stoned.+

ADVENT CANDLES

listen to the prophets speaking
speaking of a child to come
child to be both Priest and King
listen to the prophets' word

listen to the Bethlehem song
sung by all the urban-dwellers
of a child who will come
to correct every wrong

angels dancing in the flame
of a fire lit by God
angels singing of a Name
that is now Incarnate Word

shepherds come a-carolling
among the ice-bare trees
singing of the winter Child
they know is heaven's King

PATIENCE

as clay waits
for its firing
so we watch
for Christ's coming

PREPARE THE WAY

peace and justice
are the messengers
that announce
"Christ is coming!"

ELIZABETH

    Mary left yesterday, without a backward look or a wave, after almost three months. I miss her.
    We talked, cooked, and wove swaddling clothes together. Placed hands on one another's rising belly. Smiled at one another. Those special moments.
    My Zechariah – he fusses! As if this were the only baby ever born. He may be unable to speak, but it's "Put your feet up," "Don't tire yourself," "Be careful," "You shouldn't walk so much," "Don't bend," either in sign language, or notes which he keeps in his robe. He waves them at me whenever he wants.
    He would wrap me in silk and keep me indoors. I need to be alone sometimes, to ponder this child come so late in our lives.   >>>

How the child leapt when Mary came, turned and kicked within my womb! How I sang to see her, sang to the root of my soul!

I look inward more and more each day, and forward to the day I will hold my son, so certain I am this is a boy.

Mary and I - we shared our dreams, smiled as we wove (her weaving not as even as it should be, but done with love).

And now she's gone, and I wait. Sunshine streams across the room; I watch the slow movement of light. I wait to bring my child, this blessed child, into the world.+

INVITATION

come with hope
come with joy
to the birthing
of the Holy Boy

MARY'S SONG

her soul shall magnify the Lord
for she shall become
the trysting place of God

ADVENT JOURNEY

one step
at a time
through four weeks

we go into winter
blindly waiting
for the day

when light
will break
into birth

ON FIRE

let hope
glow
in your eyes

let peace
warm
heart and mind

let joy
shine
as bright flame

let love
blaze
from your heart

THE POTTER'S STORY

Such a long time ago – I saw the couple after I rode out of town on our donkey, Jedediah. I had left a basket of mugs and bowls to be sold, bought new clay, household supplies for Beulah –

Where was I? Yes – late in the day, replete with wine and olives shared with friends, half-dreaming as Jedediah plodded homeward, when I saw two shadows, thrown long towards me by the late afternoon sun.

As I came closer the girl reminded me of Beulah twenty years before, pregnant with our first: her back view thin yet obviously carrying as she walked beside the man. >>>

Their silhouettes pulled me deeper into memory: Beulah as a young woman, as a mother ... I was astray in days long gone, but as I came abreast of the couple I saw how close to term she was. I pulled on the bridle.

"Jedediah, you fool, stop when you're told!"

They looked up at me, and I knew what I must do.

"Up on Jedediah, young lady," I said, climbing down, "he's cantankerous on occasion, but he knows when to be gentle. You're coming home with me."

"There's an inn further down the road," the man said. >>>

"Never mind that, your wife needs more than an inn right now."

"We'd be grateful."

The man helped her tenderly onto Jedediah's back – she smiled down at him. Definitely a love-match! I was glad I had stopped.

As we walked home he told me they were going to Bethlehem for the census, which I'd guessed as why else would they be on the road?

Yes, I took them home for the night and Beulah fussed happily over the girl, whose name I can't remember, it's so long ago – just the outline of the couple as they walked into failing sunlight. It seemed auspicious.+

HEAR YE

prophets shout
to skiers
and snowboarders

they call
along country lanes
beside frozen lakes

seers cry
to shoppers
and salespeople

they tell
of one who is
Joy to the World

PREPARATION

mail cards
decorate the tree
wrap gifts

sweep the stable
dust the manger
lay fresh straw

then wait …
wait …
for the Birth Day

OTHER YEARS

a stack of cards on the table
waiting for wishes
to be sealed within them
while my mind wanders
to other Christmases
when children made paper chains
stirred Christmas cake
made cookies & gingerbread men
on the kitchen counter

the smell of cinnamon
the sounds of youth
anticipating joy

STILL CENTRE

weary
we stumble
out of shopping
the rush of baking
news reports of genocide
famine   pandemic
into calm
      light
a place of peace
to find
the Child

THE SHEPHERD BOY'S STORY

A couple passed me in the street today. Why I noticed them among the crowds in Bethlehem I don't know, except that she was heavily pregnant, drooping, leaning on her man. He supported her and walked anxiously, scanning the house-fronts.

I was in town getting supplies for the next week for the three of us out on the hills. I had flour, salt, and oil for the lanterns. When I saw the couple I was hurrying to get a leather strap to mend the latch on the sheepfold.

>>>

The man was a stranger, one of those here for the census, looking for a place to stay for the night, I was sure. Not much chance unless he had money to burn. I was dodging through the hordes but he caught my eyes for a moment.

I got half-way down the street – I couldn't get him, or her, out of my mind – I turned and ran back, afraid I would miss them. But I found them and grabbed his arm.

"You're looking for a place for the night?"

He nodded.

"Go to Moishe's, down there on the left, almost out of town. He might have a place for you, maybe a stable or something."

And I turned away, went on to get that strap.

The man's face haunts me. I didn't get a look at his wife.+

THE LONG WAIT

stable warm
stable bright

we'll watch
for sunset

wait for sunrise
all night long

for the Child
        to come

THE SOLDIER'S STORY

Bethlehem stinks. Too many people, too many cattle. Before Caesar Augustus ordered this census, we marched down the streets and the rabble got out of our way. We were looked up to, feared … we ruled. Now – chaos.

We're jostled and shoved by people, camels, donkeys, carts. Even beggars expect us to step round instead of them scrambling aside.

I'm tired of being asked 'Where do we register?' Men, with their swarming families, expect us to tell them where to eat, sleep, and find lost children, most of them in bad Aramaic or worse Latin. I'm a soldier, not an information post.

Today Lucas and I tried to march through town, on orders to keep discipline round one of the registration rooms where there'd been trouble last night. We were almost there when I slipped in camel dung, fell against a man, and nearly knocked him down.   >>>

I straightened up, about to pull my short sword. Horrified, and terrified, he gasped, one arm round his pregnant wife, who looked about to deliver on the street.

Frantically, he gestured to her with his free hand.

"Be careful," he gasped.

"Where are you going?" I asked. I've fathered a few in my time: he needed shelter for his wife.

"I've been told to go to the inn down the street," he said.

"We'll get you there," I said, "come on."

I went ahead, Lucas behind them, to protect them from the crowds. We pushed, shoved, yelled, ordered. People squeezed away from us.

We left them at the inn door.+

JOSEPH AND MARY

what kind of parents are you –
leaving home and family
with your first-born
ready for entrance?

father plods beside the donkey,
mother jogs on its back
        each jolt
        an ache in your body

        every night anxiety
        blows through your dreams

you didn't plan this
Rome decreed it
story tells it –
this journey
        to destiny

but – what kind of parents
        are you?

SONG FOR MARY

your love great within you
now almost full term
shifts to his birthing
as hill-town horizons

your hands to his bulking
urge peace to his movement
the journey not finished
'til lodging be found

"hush then, my unborn
hush then, within me"
motherhood cries

peace comes with your homing
as journey is ended
and love in a stable
births to sky-singing
that encompasses earth

WATCH-NIGHT

we watch the candle
burn the night
and itself

we watch the clock
turn minutes
into hours

we watch   wait
until darkness turns
to Christmas dawn

CHRISTMAS EVE

to-morrow
it seems like yesterday
you are
        you were
        born

is your birth
the one I remember
or the one that comes?

born in   out
and before   time
where reason and feeling
transcend each other
in belief

you come
        have come
        will come
no tense is perfect
to give definition
to your eternity

INTO CHRISTMAS

wind shouts through trees
fir branches banner protests
against rain

I watch behind glass
as the story storms into December
towards one Silent Night

CHRISTMAS

MAYBE THIS TIME

let it be this time
that the stable is open
within me

let it be this time
that the light is born
within me

let it be this time
that Christ is come
within me

HERE THE DAY

was a stall
was a stable
was a night

came a mother
came a father
came the night

born a child
born a King
born that night

comes a prayer
comes a song
comes a day

here the child
here the King
here the day

HOLY

Child of the universe
Maker of the stars
welcome
        to the manger

LOOKING FORWARD

lamplight shines
from a stable door
and all our paths
are bright at last

TODAY

God's kingdom come
Christ's reign begin
here this day
in every heart

THE SERVANT'S STORY

My feet hurt. And so would yours if you'd been in and out, up and down the stairs all day. The inn is packed.

"Clean this floor." "Water from the well!" Chava endlessly fussing from sunrise to past midnight.

My feet hurt and I'd like to soak them in a mustard bath but one of the men in front right is yelling for it. There're six men in one room which is meant for two. Bethlehem is like an ants' nest with the census: jammed to the skies and seething bodies, many of them drunk.

And then Moishe has to rent the stable – I ask you, the stable! – to another couple just because she's pregnant. I had to clear old straw and hay out of that rat hole. At least we've no cattle in there this week. And Chava yells for water and rags to be taken down there as if the baby were coming this minute. >>>

There's no peace in this world and here I am, taking water back there. The lane beside the inn is steep and dark and if I cut my feet I'll demand extra money for the trouble.

The man meets me at the stable-mouth, takes the water without a word of thanks. I peer in. She's in the straw alright, in the corner out of the wind, crouched and bent forward, her back to me, straining … … I get a glimpse before the man shoves me away.

There'll be a baby here tonight. And maybe I helped. Maybe the straw could have been cleaner, and maybe I should have scrubbed the manger harder. Oh well. But where there's a new baby … I've one son two years old, bless his heart, with another on the way.

I'm coming, Chava, I'm coming. But my feet hurt.+

IN THE QUIET

tonight   listen
and you will hear
Jesus come
as silence
in your prayer

tonight   listen
and you will hear
angels sing
the midnight
cold and clear

tonight   listen
and you will hear
Mary's joy
as she holds her son
close and dear

LISTEN

hear the prophets
speak of one
who comes

hear the crush
in Bethlehem's
streets

hear the shepherds
run
to worship

hear the song
that Mary
sings

THIS CHILD COMES

this Child comes
bright as a wave
breaking at night

this Child comes
forsaking majesty
dominion and power
to be a newborn
silken-skinned
vulnerable to cold
and hunger
this Almighty Child

THE STABLE'S STORY

    Smoky darkness coils in shadows. Spiders lurk in rock crevices and mice nest in corners. The couple crouches by the tiny fire away from the cave's cold mouth.

    He watches out of the corners of his eyes, trying not to see her pain as she urges the baby to birth, shifts her robe back on her thighs.

    Sweat runs on her cheeks, down her neck. He reaches out with a cloth and wipes her face. She manages a smile.

    Hours run one into one another. A servant brings water. The fire flares and dies; he feeds it to flame again. He feels the chill of the night on his skin; she seems unaware.   >>>

A thin newborn cry breaks his concentration. He has forgotten the cause of her pain, been too focused on her.

She reaches between her legs and lifts the baby from the straw. He cuts the cord, bundles the placenta away, and hands her the swaddling cloths. She wraps the baby loosely and lies back, settling him against her.

The baby turns his head into her, seeking her breast as she opens her robe. She smiles sleepily.

Gently, the father changes the straw under her, pulls her robe down round her legs. He sits beside her, touches the baby's face with a rough finger.

Light dances around them.+

FIRST CRY

I stare into the flames
watch them flicker
and see   a lantern
lighting the corner
of a stable
hear the movement
of cattle
low voices of parents
and the first cry
of a new born

OUT OF HEAVEN

far from home
family and friends
in the dark
of a lonely night
a Son is born

WONDERFUL

to us the Child is born
to us the Word is spoken

to us birth is given
into the Light of Christ

MARY PONDERS

words she holds
within her heart

her soul magnifies the Lord
for she has become
the trysting place of God

one Word she carries
in loving arms

THE CHILD'S STORY

I like babies, except when they get to be two years old like my sister. Today I heard that there's a new baby down at Moishe and Chava's inn. Born in their stable! I'm going to see him.

I slip out of the house while Mother isn't looking, dodge merchants, jump goats, duck past soldiers as I run through the streets.

At Moishe's inn, I push round a donkey, and peer through the doorway past Chava, who haggles with a man about his bill. I suck my lower lip and wrinkle my nose. I won't ask Chava if I can go to the stable, she'll say 'No'.

>>>

Round the side of the building I run, down the alley, steep, dark, and scary. There are old caves behind the inn, one with a blanket at the opening.

I lift it and slide into the smell of old manure and rotten hay. Lantern-light shines behind a screen of piled junk. I peep round the corner. A man and woman sit on the floor, talking softly. She holds the baby.

The man looks up; he doesn't seem surprised. The woman doesn't move.

I rub one foot up and down my leg, feeling shy. Then I edge closer. The baby's asleep, eyelids flickering, tiny fingers opening and closing. He's not as good looking as my sister when she was born.

He opens his eyes. It's as if the sun came out.+

MOTHER AND BABY

the wail
of a newborn
stills

as the child
is held to Mary's
breast

such is
the humanity
of God

CAROL

what story is told
this Christmas night
but of a child
born as the Light

what song is sung
this Christmas day
but of a child
born as the Way

THIS WONDER

wrapped in light
lasered down sky

to be clothed
in bone   blood

laughter   speech

and a touch of awe
this Child

DO YOU HEAR?

have you heard the sound
of shadows shattering?
bodies bending?

sounds created
by the birth of a Child
in winter

WORD

your Word comes
as a wind singing
down the wings
of the sky
shredding stolid walls
of heart and soul
until in the midst of stone
a Child is born

THIS CHRISTMAS

may I be the stable
and may the Child
be born
in my candlelight

THE SERVANT

maker of the stars
Word of the universe
now servant
to human hands

TO BETHLEHEM

homespun dark
crackling with fire
      sheep nudging stones

flames caught stars
      and flared an angel
      with us cowering

words of promise
      bannered our eyes
      a king ... in a stable

sky blazed
here to horizon
every star winged
and singing
              >>>

we ran   gravel burling
            sand scuffing
            breath heaving
            talk spurting

Bethlehem   to Bethlehem ...
to find this king
         (king? in a stable?)

low door behind an inn
new parents
with a child, an ember
cradled by the mother

her hands smouldering
about flame
light to catch
            a hilltop

THE SHEPHERD'S STORY

I stare into the flames, remember fires blazing across the sky, stars that sang a message so strange the words still echo in my head, "Peace on earth".

I touch the amulet at my neck, rub it, calling on the one God. Yet no danger came from the shining beings.

Sheep stir in the fold and I get up to look. Sit again and poke the fire. Elias snores in the shadows; the boy circles the fold, comes and sits beside me.

The hills are my help and my safety, yet from them come bears and lions that threaten, bring danger. I watch the fire, half expecting it again to swell and become huge figures dancing on the sky. The terror of the sight fills me again and I shiver, hold to God who protects me. >>>

Those great beings of light told us to go to Bethlehem ... and we went ... we ran, leaving the boy to mind the sheep. To be puzzled: we saw only a child in a stable, in a manger, cobwebs hanging, no door, yet he was lit from within ... and that is all.

A king, they said. Maybe he will be king when he is grown, but for now, despite the singing that shook the stars, he is a child. No sign of royalty, no rich robes, everything so ordinary, so poor, so like my home.+

ANGELS AND SHEPHERDS

angels fell
out of stars
into firelight

they caught
calloused voices
and held a sheepfold
in their wings

until
human fear undone
they released
the song of heaven

UNSAFE CHILD

fingers curled
in newborn sleep
this Creator of the world
has only
destiny to keep

STABLE

you are born
in our dark obscurities
not our public
"open for viewing" areas

you come
unexpected   hidden
to be swaddled in the entangling
of our love   our joy
at your so private birth

your infant light
in our darkness
thrusts out the night
to fire the stars with singing

LET US

join the angels'
white-winged prayer
"Peace on earth
goodwill to all"

GOD ON EARTH

all-aware
all-present
all-powerful
baby
in a manger

THE CAMELEER'S STORY

I lean against my master's camel in the moonlight, with that crazy star blazing overhead, convinced the whole expedition is bewitched. Whoever heard of trailing up and down mountains, crossing the desert, for months, and at this time of year, following a star?

If I weren't promised freedom at the end, I'd quit, run away. I'm sick of ailing camels, fractious donkeys ... and of being afraid.

Yes, afraid – of where this journey is going to end, if it does, and scared of the night.

Scared of the star that turns the desert white where it should be dark ... and throws shadows across the sky.

It's fine for the masters to be certain of what they're doing, busy with charts and calculations; we slaves have to do what we're told and no questions.

>>>

I'm longing for freedom when we get home – if we get home.

Brigands in the mountains, dust storms in the desert with freezing nights and thieves – I knifed one last week. He was stealing my heavy cloak.

I saw him moving away from the camels. At first I thought he'd killed my master's camel but she grunted so I ran after the man, knife in hand. I caught him behind and thrust the knife into his back. Then I dragged him behind a cairn, to survive or not. He wasn't there in the morning.

We always leave before dawn, rest in the heat of the day, and travel late in the night so that we don't wander from the arc of the star. That star sees everything.+

TRADITION

hangs scarlet bows
on branches
rimed with frost

colours each day
with small pictures
and cedar branches

plays carols
over and over
wraps presents

tells familiar stories
year after year
round the manger

THE STRANGER

comes a Stranger
to the stable
small and fragile
to be cradled
in ornament
and evergreen

comes a Stranger
in the darkness
singing carols
bright with glory
while an angel
lifts her trumpet

comes the Stranger
to the winter
of our world
offers news
of peace and joy
with open hands

CHAVA'S STORY

At last. I can sit down. The final guest has registered for the census and gone. The inn is empty for the moment. Moishe will grumble about no income, but we made plenty over these months.

Bethlehem was full to bursting. People slept on roofs, in the street, in doorways, anywhere they could. We had rooms filled to overflowing, the place echoed with snores at night.

I'm so tired, my back and legs ache.

I kept a lentil stew on the stove day and night, never knowing what to expect.

At least it was never dull: we had fights; men who paid double; money stolen; people who 'forgot' to pay; children lost; and a baby born out in the stable.

>>>

That stable. I thought Moishe had lost his mind, though he didn't charge the parents much.

He said the baby was coming so I sent a servant down with water. I wanted to help but there was an accident and burns to anoint.

I never did see the baby. Moishe said a few shepherds came to see him … at least someone welcomed the poor child. What a place to be born, what a beginning.+

IN CHRISTMAS

in you   our Christmas carols
            are singing
        one perfect harmony

in you   the Christmas star
            is shining
        to give us holy light

in you   our Christmas gifts
            all become
        one precious holy gift

in you   the Christmas créche
            is focused
        as one perfect vision

EPIPHANY

CHRISTMAS QUESTIONS

how many roads
lead to Bethlehem
where the Prince of Peace lies
wrapped in stars?

how many people
walk to Bethlehem
to cradle the Prince of Peace
in hands of praise?

how many stars
light the winter sky
when the Prince of Peace sings
with angel choirs?

A POEM FOR CHRISTMAS

where should I leave
the poem I carved
and carried from the east?

shall I set it
in a niche
framed in velvet?

or lay it in straw
at a manger's edge
and watch stars dance
at its hallowing?

AND NOW

He is presented
as Light
to all nations
and Friend
to all people

NEXT TIME

we watch and wait
and cannot know
the day or hour
when God will come
                    again

HEROD

I am The King. There is no other King but me. I have rebuilt the Temple, placated foreign gods, created Caesarea and its great new harbour. I have built this palace, rebuilt the Antonia fortress … my kingship is absolute, and respected by the Emperor.

Those three magi from the East, with their story of another 'king' whose star they have followed from the East… they will return to me, for I am Herod The King.

I have invited them back to Jerusalem to attend a feast in their honour. There will be veiled dancers and musicians. And they will tell me where to find this 'king' both in gratitude and as between one lord and another, though I am the greater.

And I will find this king ….

Nothing shall threaten my rule over Judah. My children tried – and they were executed, as was fitting.+

THE ANSWER

can the sword cut
between law and justice?

will soldiers kill
the voice of peace?

does a dictator rule
the voice of love?

only the Child's hands
can cleanse the night

WISE MEN

they knelt,
set aside their crowns
laid down their gifts
of pride, greed, power
before they put down
the gold, frankincense, myrrh

in this
lay wisdom

CONSIDERING GIFTS

shall I offer words hanging
like wisps of straw
to warm the child
in smoky darkness

can I give
a scarf to warm
the homeless parent

fill an empty belly
that the wanderer
may sleep soundly

should I bring
a dog to comfort
loneliness

BEYOND EPIPHANY

star
above
a stable
signals the Child
to foreign magi
who carry the Christ-Light
to their own communities

BLESSED

creek and tree
sand and sky
barnacle and bird
woven in
the tapestry of creation

blessed in lantern light
by newborn hands

CHRISTMAS LIGHT

one small light
in stable dark
flows far and wide
to every heart

SHINING

conceived of light
who was to be
Light for the world
and is, forever
Light with us

TOLD AGAIN

the story circles
in firelight
spirals out
on angel wings
settles
on a hammer
on a hill-top

but it began
far Away
in a Manger

STAR-KISSED

a star
betrayed you
to the universe
when it kissed
watching kings

it nailed a sign
on hill-town walls
"This is
the King of the Jews"

the star winked and died
when it saw the life
it had foresworn

COME EARLY

arise and come
with the wise ones
to worship
the Lord

VOCATION

called from worship
into action
we move beyond the limit
of our hands.

INCOMPLETE CHRISTMAS

I promise myself a complete Christmas
prayer-wrapping for each gift
and praise sparkling on the tree

but I read about Syria
count food-bank listings
while AIDS is epidemic in Africa

prayer folds over darkness
praise wraps canned foods
and a manger fills with tears

CHRISTMAS ON THE RUN

I tried to hold Christmas in place
        angels flew too fast
        shepherds took to the hills
        kings returned
        to homes in the east

I was left on a hillside
with a sky of stars
        and three trees

BEGINNING

morning ascends
in the fire of a Mexican sun
to burn preconceptions
in resurrection

sing   sky   tell the world
we are to be
new   changed
by birth in an old land

herald us   angels
as we come to be born
in a stable

THE SLAVE'S STORY

They came out of the stable with their crowns in their hands, in a glow of light, of peace, of silence. Then Caspar, my master, said, "We'll go south, then east."

Melchior asked, "We don't return to Herod?"

"Definitely not," said Balthazar.

That was all the discussion they had before mounting their camels. Our caravan moved off swiftly, south.

The magi said little as we travelled that day. Once Caspar said, "His life is in danger." No one answered. I'm puzzled: what kind of protection does a child need, born in a stable?

I thought kings lived in palaces like the rulers of my masters' kingdom, like Herod. I thought they had trains of camels, horses, slaves, like the magi. Now I don't know what to think. >>>

We had followed a blazing star across deserts and mountain ranges to see this king. We brought rich gifts which had always to be guarded, gifts fit for a king.

Yet they found this king in a stable. I thought they'd cast around, ask for directions, to find the real king. Yet they went in, robed in silks and velvets. And stayed an hour or more.

What kind of king is born in a stable? What *is* a king? I thought I knew, but I don't.+

ONGOING

a shepherd carries a candle
down the length of dark
to fire the stars
and Christmas is again

a king carries myrrh
down desert nights
following a star
and the message
is told again

a child takes light
through winter days
out from the stable
and the world
is bright again

CHRISTMAS CHILD

by faith
we hold
and know
the fragility
of God

GIFT FROM GOD

with an hallelujah of angels
you give us
your life

with our two hands
we offer you
our hearts

THE MOMENT

we come
into the light
from darkness

pause before
the Child
his parents

kneel in wonder
with empty hands
full heart

WELCOME

lamplight shines
from the stable door

and a child

guides shepherd
king and slave
to coronation

RETURN

the story tells
and retells

the angels sing
year after year

the child comes again
and again

THE FUTURE

a child peers
out of the darkness

catches tinsel in one hand
paper hats in the other

swings on a fancy chain
until it breaks

and the child tumbles
into a dangerous life

STARLIGHT

a single light
carried with care
passed flame
by flame
to the homeless
hungry and lonely
that they be warmed
comforted
and given peace
In the Bleak
Midwinter

THE MAGUS

What happens now? And what happened then?

We followed the star, not 'a star' but *the* star, from its rising to the place of its settling: over a stable in Bethlehem, a small town in Judea.

We found, not the king we expected, but a king nevertheless.

A rough journey – cantankerous slaves, a stolen camel - and an ending beleaguered by a trial of wits with Herod. We out-foxed him for, between ourselves, we would not return to tell him of the child.

A week ago, in all humility, we laid our gifts before such shining light, light that shimmered, reached up and out, and touched our guiding star.

And now? Who do we tell? Who will believe? And *what* do we tell? That we saw a king, whose kingdom is not of this world but of some radiant place not marked on our maps. >>>

I ponder these things, and find no answers in charts, or my thoughts, which range over stories of the creation of the world, to questions such as: How does one weigh a flame? How does one portray a voice on a scroll? Where is wisdom found? From whence comes the power of a child's fingers?

The child's radiance is great within me; I feel and fear it.

My camel strides onward, the saddle creaks, harness jingles, slaves mutter around me. My two companions watch the turn of land, and say little.

Answers lie in the light shining from that child, and I understand them not. But somehow the answer is within.+

ACKNOWLEDGEMENTS

These poems and stories have appeared in my two chapbooks, *Watch Night* and *This Holy Night*. Many of them have appeared in the Parish Magazine of St. John the Baptist Anglican Church, Cobble Hill, B.C., many are new, others have appeared on my blog:
http://www.1960willowtree.wordpress.com/
or in *Canta, Celebrating-a-round, Christmas Blessings, Cuernavaca Diary, The Diocesan Post, The Eagle, Living Message, Never Bury Poetry, Purpose, Time of Singing,* and *Writer's Own Magazine.*

JOANNA M. WESTON. Married; has two cats, multiple spiders, a herd of deer, and two derelict hen-houses. Her middle-reader, 'Frame and The McGuire', published by Tradewind Books; and poetry, 'A Summer Father', published by Frontenac House of Calgary. Her eBooks found at her blog: http://www.1960willowtree.wordpress.com/

Made in the USA
Columbia, SC
09 September 2018